This Story Book
Belongs to

_____

On the following pages
write your own stories, based
on the pictures shown.
Answer the questions on the
prompt pages. Color in the
characters.
There is no wrong or right
way to complete this, this is
your story book.
Name your characters,
design your plot and start.

Who wrote Native Son?

_____

_____

_____

Who was Constance Baker Motley?

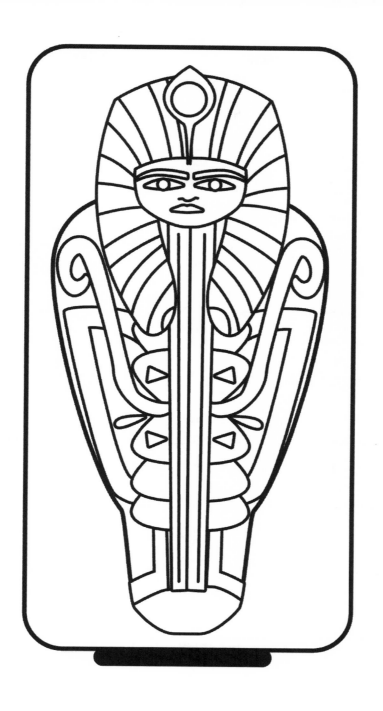

Who was Emmet Till?

Where was Malcolm X killed?

Who was "Blind Tom"?

_____

_____

_____

In what store was the first sit in at a segregated
lunch counter? (The Date was 2/1/60)

_____

_____

_____

Who was the first African American astronaut in space?

Who was Arthur Ashe?

According to records what was the highest
population of slavery in the U.S.?

Who was John Baxter Taylor Jr.?

Who was the first African American Major League Baseball Player?

(blank drawing box)

(writing lines)

What was the symbol of The Lowndes County
Freedom Organization? "I know Why the Caged Bird
Sings" was written by who?

Who was Stokely Carmichael?

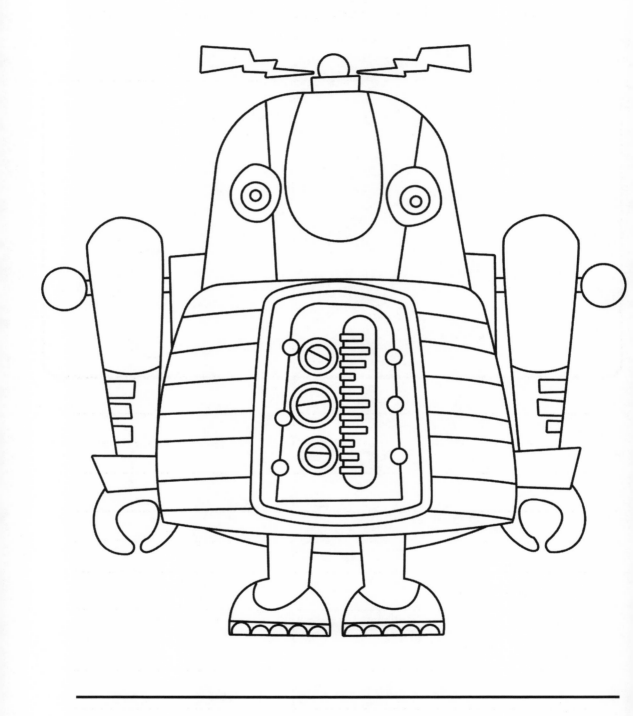

Who was the first African American to appear on a U.S. Postage Stamp?

On the following pages, trace the designs, name the place or thing, then color them in.

Then write a story about the picture after you color it.

Who were the Brotherhood of Sleeping Car Porters & what did they do?

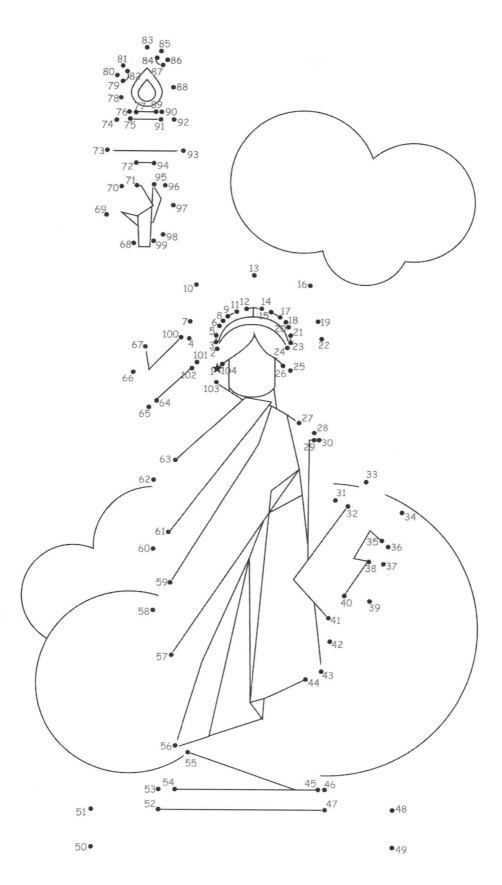

Who was the first African American to serve as a U.S. Senate?

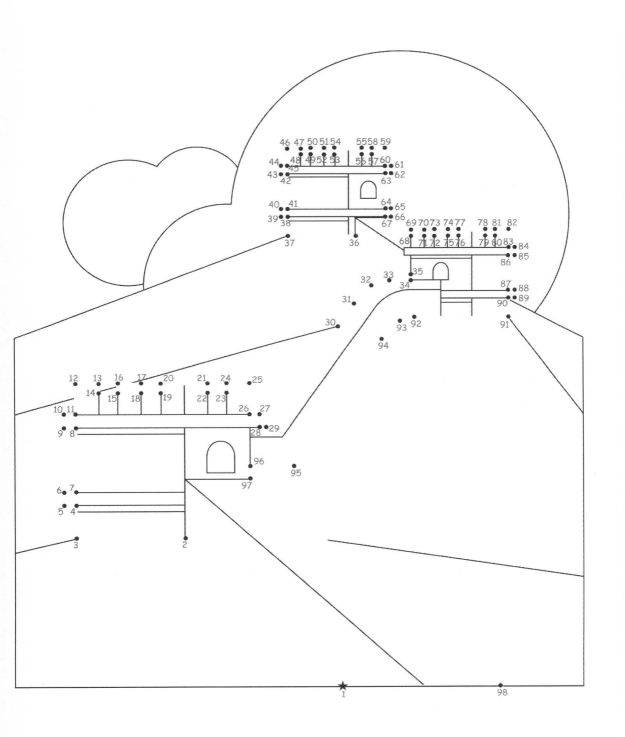

What is Executive Order 9981 & who signed it?

Who was Carl Stokes?

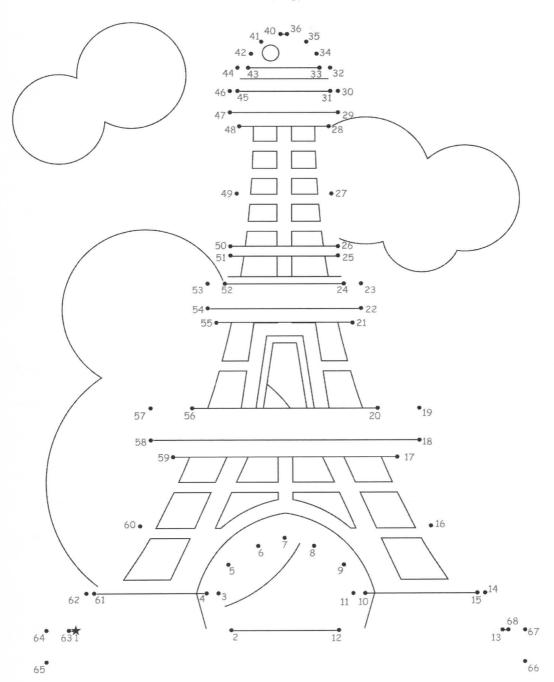

Who was Hattie Mcdaniel?

Who was Garrett Morgan? What are two things that he did?

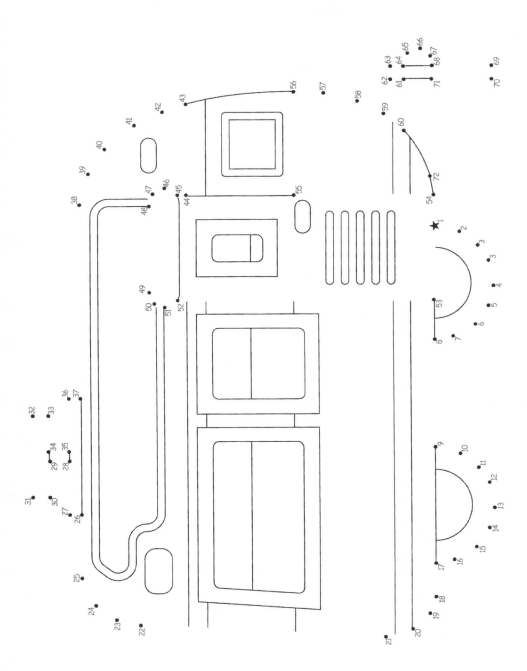

Who shot Martin Luther King?

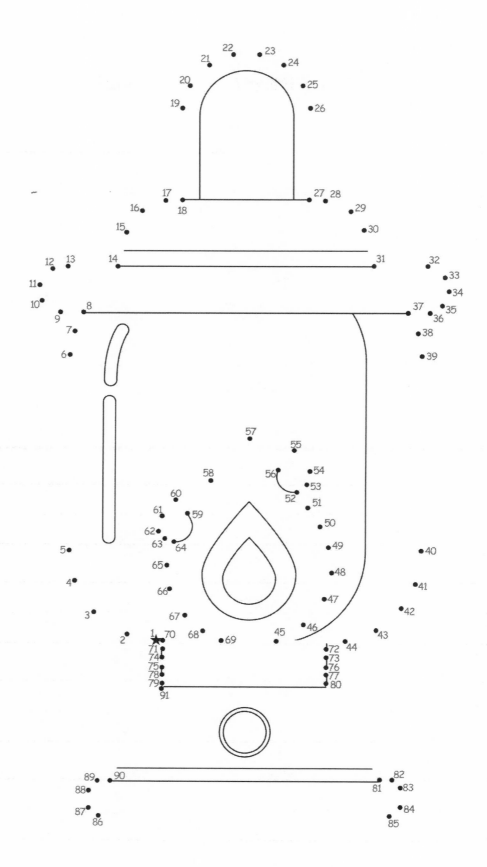

Who was Henry "Box" Brown?

Who was the first African American Noble Peace Prize Winner?

Who was the first African American member of the PGA? Who was Jean Baptiste Pointe Du Sable?

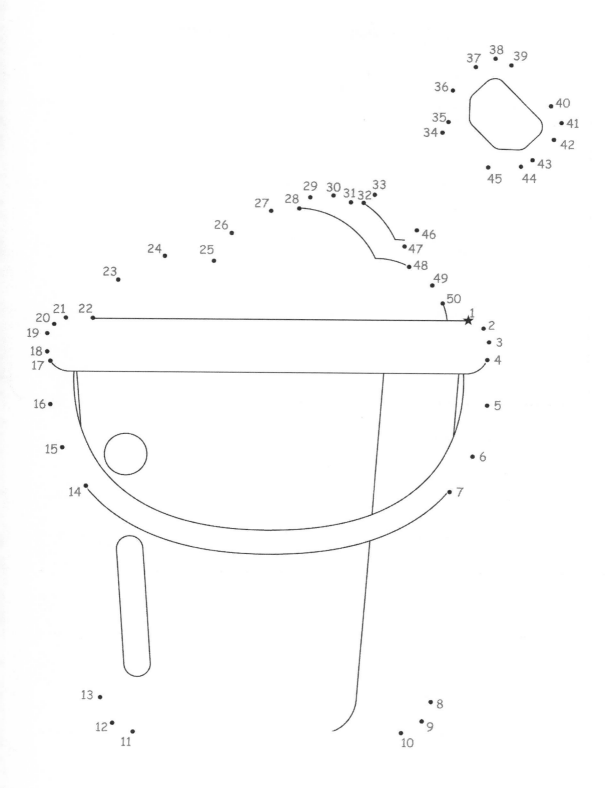

What liberties did the 15th Amendment give African Americans?

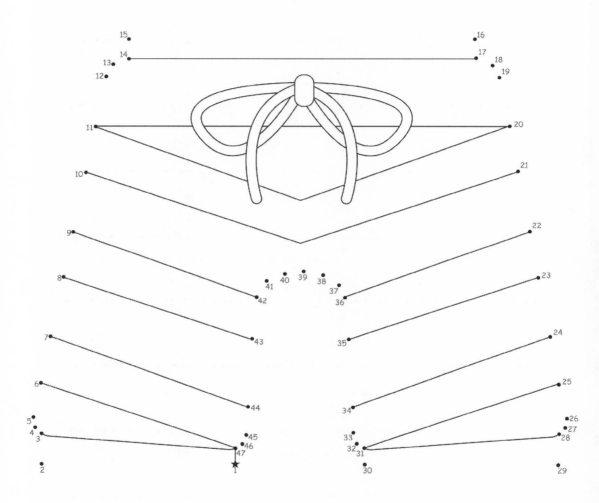

Who was the first African American to serve as a U.S. Supreme Court Justice?

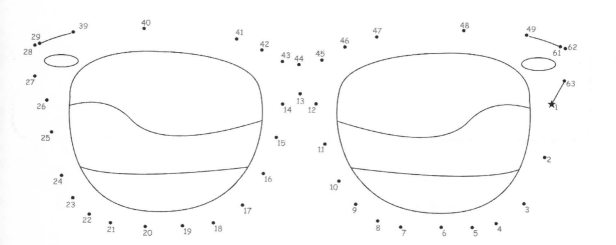

What liberties did the 13th Amendment give African Americans?

Who was Richard Theodore Greener?

Who was Daniel Hale Williams & what did he do?

The End!

Made in the USA
Middletown, DE
11 December 2019

80465694R00057